Daisy Maria S. Chiareli Vallim

Analysing Audit Reports

Daisy Maria S. Chiareli Vallim

Analysing Audit Reports

Popular Pharmacy Programme

ScienciaScripts

Cover image: www.ingimage.com

This book is a translation from the original published under ISBN 978-613-9-63517-7.

Publisher:
Sciencia Scripts
is a trademark of
Dodo Books Indian Ocean Ltd. and OmniScriptum S.R.L publishing group

120 High Road, East Finchley, London, N2 9ED, United Kingdom
Str. Armeneasca 28/1, office 1, Chisinau MD-2012, Republic of Moldova, Europe
Printed at: see last page
ISBN: 978-620-7-66749-9

THANKS

To the State University of Ceará, especially the employees of the Brazilian Nursing Association Ceará section, ABEn - CE, who provided all the conditions to achieve this achievement.

To my parents, José Wilson da Silva and Maria Daci Silva, for supporting my dreams and paying for my studies, giving me the opportunity to obtain the title of Specialist in Management, Auditing and Expertise in Health Systems.

To my brothers, Thiago, Liduina and Verônica (In Memorian), for the happy moments shared and for supporting my studies.

To all the professors of the Postgraduate Course in the Specialization Course in Management, Auditing and Expertise in Health Systems at the State University of Ceará, for the excellent academic training provided.

To my love, Thiago Chiareli Vallim, for the happy moments shared, even though I was far away, your love, your affection, your sincerity and your simplicity won me over and in sharing these feelings, I offer my true love.

To my dearest friend and sister, Amanda Holanda Severo, for the teachings shared.

To my friends, Amanda, Arthur, Giselle, Lorenna, Mansueto, Thiago, Yasmin and Zélia who are part of the family I chose, remaining by my side at all times.

SUMMARY

The VIII National Health Conference was a rehearsal for the creation of the Unified Health System, which was created in the 1988 constitution, with equity, universality, decentralization and integrality as its principles. Given the scope of a single and universal health system, it is necessary to incorporate strategies to improve the system, auditing is one of the tools used to improve the system. Considering the relevance of the theme and the tiny number of studies on the audit, interest arose in developing a documentary study having as its guiding thread the analysis of the audit reports of the Farmácia Popular do Brasil program in the city of Fortaleza in the period from 2010 to 2014. The present study aims to analyze these reports. This is a documentary and retrospective study. The selected material was collected electronically at the Ministry of Health/ Secretary of Strategic and Participatory Management/ National Audit Department of the Unified Health System. The following inclusion criteria were used: being an audit activity report; having been carried out in the municipality of Fortaleza-CE; focus on the Brazilian Popular Pharmacy Program; having been carried out between 2010 and 2014. Thus, there were a total of eight reports, namely: Audit N° 10727; Audit No. 11357; Audit No. 11358; Audit No. 11527; Audit No. 12401; Audit N° 12406 and Audit N° 12912. The ethical aspects in the research were respected at all stages, in accordance with the requirements established in Resolution 466/12 of the National Health Council. The results were divided into two moments, the first, the characterization of the audit, the executing body and location, the purpose of the audit, the phases and date of execution, the applicant, as well as the form and object of the audit were addressed. The second moment, the audit findings, this item addressed identifications, findings/evidence, compliance and compliance. The two moments were analyzed separately by audit reports. Considering the irregularities presented in the audit reports analyzed, compensation was recommended to the Ministry of Health. Based on the facts presented , it can be concluded that many managers have little knowledge of the laws/decrees/ordinances in force. It is necessary to raise awareness, train managers and staff through higher health bodies and encourage the practice of continuing education so that they can carry out their activities, correctly complying with everything established by law.

Keywords: Nursing audit. Health Unic System. Health services administration.

SUMMARY

CHAPTER 1

INTRODUCTION

The federal constitution of 1888 brought great gains to the population, including the Unified Health System (SUS). Articles 193 to 200 deal with health as a right for everyone and a duty of the state. The ideas presented at the VIII National Health Conference in 1986 discussed a health reform including principles of equity, universality, decentralization and comprehensiveness, thus offering the creation of the first universal public health system in Brazil (BARBOSA, 2013).

The health reform that was carried out with a view to creating the SUS, implemented in the Constitution, was in fact a break with all the principles that had governed health policy until then. And in this sense we can actually talk about ideological and institutional reordering. Ideological due to the guiding principles of the foundation and function of health policy in Brazil, which were completely changed, and institutional due to the creation/structure of the single system (MENICUCCI, 2014).

The official regulation of the SUS occurred in 1990, through Organic Health Law No. 8,080/90. Since then, several norms, guidelines, laws, decrees and ordinances have followed, dealing with various aspects of management and financing, with the aim of guaranteeing the compliance with its principles. The SUS completed 25 years in 2013, representing a historic milestone in the Brazilian reality, both from the perspective of health management and public health administration.

According to Claudino (2013), auditing is adopted as a tool for controlling costs and evaluating the quality of healthcare. Since then, the practice of health auditing has expanded, being adopted in the public sector as an essential tool for controlling and regulating the use of health services and, in the private sector, as an instrument for controlling the costs of care provided. to the patient.

Given the scope of a single and universal health system, it is necessary to incorporate strategies to improve the system. The Health Pact is an instrument that will produce significant changes in SUS regulations and comprises three dimensions - Pact for Life, Pact in Defense of SUS and Management Pact. Its purpose is to qualify the public management of the SUS, seeking greater effectiveness, efficiency and quality of its responses.

The Pact is the result of many discussions since 2003, when the National Council of State Health Secretaries (CONASS) requested the Ministry of Health (MS) to review the SUS regulatory processes.

The managers understood that the SUS regulations should take into account the heterogeneity of Brazil and new regulations/ordinances/decrees/laws would have to take into account the principles of the SUS, under the aegis of health responsibility, appropriate to the reality of each State and region of the country, integrating health promotion actions, primary care, medium and high complexity care, epidemiology and disease control, health and environmental surveillance; the reaffirmation of the importance of the deliberative bodies of the Bipartite Inter-Management Commission (CIB) and the Tripartite Inter-Management Commission (CIT) and the strengthening of social control (MACHADO et al, 2009).

The 2006 Health Pact reinforces solidarity and cooperation between spheres of government, defining health responsibilities, creating spaces for co-management and rescuing support between entities in a shared process. In this sense, auditing as a management instrument in the context of a Health System also assumes the mission of evaluating the efficiency, effectiveness, effectiveness and economicity of health actions and services, providing technical cooperation and proposing corrective measures, subsidizing the planning and monitoring with validated and reliable information (MINISTÉRIO DA SAÚDE, 2011).

Each and every service provision must have as its principle the quality of service and the product/input offered to its clientele, so in healthcare we have the same principle.

To monitor this quality in healthcare, it is necessary to use quality tools. One of the most efficient ways to monitor a management system is the audit, as, when well applied, it diagnoses non-conformities in the evaluated service, being carried out by trained professionals who present, in addition to technical-scientific knowledge, personal attributes such as impartiality, prudence and diplomacy. , through opinions based on laws, ordinances, decrees, resolutions (AYACH et al., 2013).

The audit is an important tool in the transformation of work processes that have been taking place in hospitals and health plan operators, which are seeking to restructure themselves to maintain the quality of care provided and at the same time guarantee a competitive position in the healthcare market. work (DIAS et al, 2011).

In view of the above, considering the relevance of the theme and the tiny number of studies on auditing, the interest in developing a documentary study with the analysis of audit reports from the Farmácia Popular do Brasil program in the city of Fortaleza in the period of 2010 to 2014.

With the focus on quality care and increased competitiveness among organizations that provide health services, opportunities are increasingly emerging for professional nurses to work in the auditing area. In this way, the audit is configured as a management tool used by health professionals, especially nurses, with the purpose of evaluating non-conformities in the analyzed service.

CHAPTER 2

THEORETICAL SUPPORT

2.1 HISTORY OF AUDIT IN SUS

Auditing had its origins in the accounting area, whose facts and records date back to 2,600 years before Christ. However, it was from the 12th century after Christ that this technique began to be called auditing, with its greatest development occurring in England with the Industrial Revolution.

The word audit originates from the Latin audire which means to listen. However, the term can be better explained by the English word audit, which has the meaning of examining, correcting and certifying. Therefore, the audit consists of the systematic and formal evaluation of an activity to determine whether it is being carried out in accordance with its objectives (DIAS et al, 2011).

In this way, the practice of auditing received new guidelines in the search to meet the needs of large companies, emerging in the health area and thus appears for the first time in the work carried out by the doctor George Gray Ward, in the United States in 1918, in this work , it verifies the quality of assistance provided to the client, through records in the medical record (BRASIL, 2003).

Auditing activities, before 1976, based on the then National Institute of Social Security (INPS), were carried out by supervisors through investigations into patient records and hospital accounts. At the time, there were no direct audits in hospitals.

From 1976 onwards, the so-called hospital bills became the Hospital Admission Guide (GIH). Audit activities are established as Formal and Technical Control. In 1978, the Medical Assistance Secretariat was created, subordinate to the National Institute of

Social Security Medical Assistance (INAMPS). There was a need to improve the GIH. The Control and Evaluation Coordination was then created - in the capitals, and the Social Medicine Service - in the municipalities (BRASIL, 2003).

In 1983, the Hospital Admission Authorization (AIH), replaced the GIH, in the Social Security Medical Assistance System (SAMPS), in the same year, it recognized the role of doctor-auditor and the audit began to be carried out in the hospitals themselves.

In health, audits can be carried out in various sectors and by different professionals, with medical, nursing and dental audits standing out among them (AYACH et al., 2013).

The Federal Constitution of 1988 provides in its article 197: "Health actions and services are of public relevance, and it is up to the public authorities to provide, under the terms of the Law, on their regulation, supervision and control, and their execution must be carried out directly or through of third parties and also by an individual or legal entity governed by private law" (BRASIL, 1988).

Law No. 8,080, of September 19, 1990, by providing for the creation of the National Audit System (SNA), establishes the SUS management bodies to monitor, control and evaluate health actions and services, being reserved for Union the exclusive competence to "establish the National Audit System, and coordinate the technical and financial evaluation of the SUS throughout the national territory in technical cooperation with states, municipalities and the Federal District" (BRASIlL, 1990).

Social participation proved to be essential and inherent to the process of fighting for Brazilian Health Reform and as a consequence of this fight, the constitutional right to society's participation in the SUS was guaranteed, and later expanded with the creation of the Secretariat for Strategic and Participatory Management of the SUS (SGEP) (MINISTRY OF HEALTH, 2011).

As it deals specifically with the health area, the SNA, established by article 6 of Law 8,689, of July 27, 1993 and regulated by Decree no. 1,651/95, constitutes an atypical, unique, differentiated system, complementary to the systems of internal and external control and mainly legitimate. Decree No. 1,651 of September 29, 1995:

> *"Art. 4° The SNA comprises the bodies that are established at each level of government, under the supervision of the respective management of the SUS, section § 3° The structure and functioning of the SNA, at the federal level, are indicative of the organization to be be observed by States, Federal District and Municipalities to achieve the same objectives within the scope of their respective actions* (BRASIL, 1995)

Law No. 10,683, of May 28, 2003, provides for the Organization of the Presidency of the Republic and the Ministries - it establishes in paragraph "b", item XX of article 27, as the area of competence of the Ministry of Health: "a coordination and supervision of the SUS" (BRASIL, 2003).

With the publication of Decree no. 6,860, of May 27, 2009, the SUS National Audit Department (DENASUS) became part of the structure of the Secretariat for Strategic and Participatory Management, a unique body of the Ministry of Health that gained a new format in view of the increasing degree of complexity of institutionalization of the SUS, concomitantly with the progressive decentralization of responsibilities for the execution of health actions and the use of financial resources, making it necessary to consolidate competence in the execution of the system's strategic and participatory management processes (BRASIL, 2006).

In 2006, the Health Pact, published in Ordinance No. 399, of February 22, 2006, contemplating the pact signed between health care managers

SUS, in its three dimensions, for Life, in Defense of SUS and Management. There were significant changes to the implementation of the SUS, among which we highlight: the replacement of the then qualification process with joint adherence to the Terms of Management Commitment; Solidarity and cooperative

Regionalization as a structuring axis of the Decentralization process; the Integration of the various forms of transfer of federal resources; and the Unification of the various previously existing pacts (MINISTÉRIO DA SAÚDE, 2011).

2.2 DENASUS

The National Audit Department of the Unified Health System (DENASUS) is the central coordinating body (federal sphere) of the SNA and has deconcentrated units in all units of the Federation. DENASUS is responsible for carrying out audits and strengthening the state and municipal components of the SNA of the SUS.

DENASUS aims to unify work processes and practices for the three federative entities, as well as contribute to the organizational, normative and human resources improvement of the bodies that make up the SNA, this occurs through devices that seek greater interaction and exchange of information between its components, enabling a more accurate diagnosis of development needs and human resources training actions to accept responsibilities at each level of management (MINISTÉRIO DA SAÚDE, 2014).

2.3 AUDIT AS A MANAGEMENT INSTRUMENT

Decree No. 1,171, of July 22, 1994, referring to the Code of Professional Ethics of Civil Servants of the Federal Executive Branch, in its chapter I, in section I, determines that dignity, decorum, zeal and effectiveness are recommended moral principles that should guide the health auditor. The public servant, in the role of auditor, must strive for ethics in his conduct, based on the principles of integrity, prudence, professional care and social responsibility (MINISTÉRIO DA SAÚDE, 2011).

The process of changing auditing practices, from a health perspective, incorporates the assessment of the quality of promotion, prevention and assistance actions, especially aiming to reduce inequities, guarantee the right to access and the efficiency of actions and services. This measurement takes place through health indicators and the effectiveness of participation and social control, without compromising its other functions (MINISTÉRIO DA SAÚDE, 2011).

The audit's commitment to strengthening management is established by guiding the manager regarding the efficient application of the health budget, which should reflect the improvement of epidemiological and social well-being indicators, access and humanization of services (MINISTÉRIO DA SAÚDE, 2011).

Health auditors seek the agility of interventions in the process, the identification of priorities and the organization of the health system, based on the logic of the needs of the population and not of the service provider, being a control system that informs the administration about the efficiency of programs under development. The skills of a health auditor encompass the actions of indicating problems and failures, they point out suggestions and solutions, thus assuming an educational character.

This new audit paradigm requires professionals working within the logic of a social observatory for SUS resolving issues, aiming to effectively contribute to the construction of the model it proposes, in the breadth of the health concept: quality of life and citizenship. Understanding the importance of consolidating the relationship with social control, as a way of better taking care of SUS management, the audit must carry out technical cooperation actions with municipal, state and national health councils and also with managers, in the three spheres management (MINISTRY OF HEALTH, 2011).

The objective is that together they support the qualification of management through shared information and agreed actions, in order to guide, collaborate, correct improprieties, prevent irregularities, evaluate the impact of actions, resulting in the improvement of public health management, integrating a network that reflects user satisfaction and improving the population’s quality of life (MINISTÉRIO DA SAÚDE, 2011).

2.4 POPULAR PHARMACY

The Brazilian Popular Pharmacy Program (PFPB) was created based on a demand from the Federal Government for a recommendation to expand access to medicines, a suggestion that was made through studies in large cities, with a large portion of the population using private services, but with difficulty accessing medicines. The proposal for supplying medicines at low cost used by the Pharmaceutical Laboratory of Pernambuco (LAFEPE) since 2001 began to serve as a model for the Federal Government's new initiative (PINTO et al, 2011).

In view of the findings of these studies, the Federal Government, through the Ministry of Health (MS), has implemented actions that seek to promote the expansion of the population's access to medicines, as a strategic input for Health Policies. The PFPB was characterized by the partnership between Ministry of Health and Oswaldo Cruz Foundation (Fiocruz), which began to fulfill the role of executor of the Program.

Law No. 10,858/04 authorizes the Oswaldo Cruz Foundation (FIOCRUZ) to distribute medicines, upon reimbursement of their costs, with a view to ensuring access to medicines for the population, including those currently served in supplementary healthcare (BRAZIL, 2004b). The reimbursement of costs covered by the Law is different from commercial sales, in that it does not aim to make a profit for the program units, nor for those who maintain them (BRASIL, 2005).

According to the Resolution of the Collegiate Board (RDC) National Health Surveillance Agency (ANVISA) no. 338 (BRASIL, 2004d) the peculiarities of the Brazilian pharmaceutical market have a relevant impact on the process of elaboration and execution of public policies, mainly in Pharmaceutical Assistance (AF). Studies point to the need to adopt an inclusion mechanism, resulting in expanded access to medicines and PA.

Within the scope of the SUS, Pharmaceutical Assistance's primary objective is to guarantee the continuous supply and rational use of medicines in Basic Health Units (UBS), through selection, programming, acquisition, storage, prescription and dispensing processes (FOPPA et al, 2008).

In 2004, the Federal Government launched the Popular Pharmacy Program of Brazil (PFPB). The Program emerged as a strategy to expand access, simultaneously calling into question the effectiveness of decentralization of (AF), returning to the model of centralized purchasing of medicines that has proven to be efficient for Programs under the responsibility of the Federal Government (COSTA; CASTRO, 2011). In 2006, the dispensing of medicines was expanded to supplementary health.

In this context, the Popular Pharmacy Program of Brazil was created, through Decree No. 5,090/04 (BRASIL, 2004a), whose main focus **is the expansion of the "Farmácia Popular do Brasil" network in partnership with** State and Municipal Governments (BRASIL, 2005).

The main objective of the PFPB is to make available, through reimbursement of their cost, medicines produced by state laboratories and, additionally, medicines from the private sector, focusing on the effective provision of Pharmaceutical Assistance (BRASIL, 2005).

With decentralization, the responsibility for guaranteeing access to certain groups of medicines was divided between spheres of government (COSTA; CASTRO, 2011) .

CHAPTER 3

GOALS

3.1 Main goal

A Analyze the audit reports of the Farmácia Popular do Brasil program in the municipality of Fortaleza in accordance with legal precepts.

3.2 Specific objectives

✓ Identify the main non-conformities found;

C Confront non-conformities with legal precepts;

D Describe the main recommendations established in the reports.

CHAPTER 4

METHODOLOGY

4.1 KIND OF STUDY

This is a documentary and retrospective study. Documentary research is a method that uses original documents that have not yet received analytical treatment by any author, thus differing from bibliographical research. Authors use it in an attempt to solve a problem or acquire knowledge from the information arising from the materials under study, whether graphic, sound or computerized (POLIT, 2011).

Retrospective research is a study designed to explore facts from the past, and can be designed to mark a point in the past and conduct research up to the present moment, through documentary analysis, as happens in a retrospective cohort or historical cohort study (MARCONI; LAKATOS, 2005).

4.2 SCENARIO AND SAMPLE

The selected material was collected electronically, sna.saude.gov.br/con_auditoria.cfm, at Mistério da Saúde (MS)/ Secretariat of Strategic and Participatory Management (SGEP)/ National Audit Department of the Unified Health System (DENASUS).

To select the material, the following inclusion criteria were used: being an audit activity report; having been carried out in the municipality of Fortaleza-CE; focus on the Brazilian Popular Pharmacy Program (PFPB); having been carried out between 2010 and 2014. Therefore, all other materials that did not meet these criteria were excluded.

Thus, there were a total of eight reports that met the established criteria.

These reports were: Audit report No. 10727; Audit No. 11357; Audit No. 11358; Audit No. 11527; Audit
No. 12401; Audit No. 12406 and Audit No. 12912.

4.3 DATA COLLECT

Data collection initially took place by searching for SMS audit reports on the DENASUS website. With the previously selected reports, a file was created in order to highlight the main information contained in the report in order to facilitate its analysis. From that moment on, tables containing information were created to meet the objectives of this study.

4.4 DATA ANALYSIS

The original reports were analyzed based on the constructed instrument (Appendix A), containing three items, divided into: 1. Identification data; 2. Basic data and 3. Findings. The first item included the audit number, the municipality, the state where the audit was carried out and the unit audited; the second item covered the purpose, phases, applicant, forms and object of the audit; and the third item included the number of the finding, the item, the written finding, the evidence found, the compliance and the justification. The data were analyzed according to the findings present in each report, supported by a critical-dialectical framework, current legislation and recommendations present in the reports.

4.5 ETHICAL ASPECTS

Ethical aspects in the research were respected at all stages, in accordance with the requirements established in Resolution 466/12 of the National Health Council (BRASIL, 2012).

CHAPTER 5

RESULTS AND DISCUSSIONS

According to the research carried out on the DENASUS website, and using the steps already described in the methodology, seven audit reports from the Programa Farmácia Popular do Brasil of Fortaleza-CE were used, covering the period from 2010 to 2014. The results are presented in two topics, namely: characterization of reports and audit findings. These reports were analyzed and their main characteristics are presented in the tables below. The numerous findings present in each report were presented separately by subtopics for better visualization and understanding.

5.1 CHARACTERIZATION OF AUDITS

The audit reports below are characterized in different tables that describe the following data: the executing body and location, the purpose of the audit, the phases and date of execution, the applicant, as well as the form and object of the audit.

Table 1 - Identification and basic data from audit No. 10727 of the Farmácia Popular do Brasil Program in the city of Fortaleza-CE.

AUDIT NO.: 10727		
Identification data		
Unit: Santa Branca Pharmaceutical LTDA	Municipality: Fortaleza	State: Ceará
Basic data		
Purpose: Audit of the Brazilian Popular Pharmacy Program		
Phase: Execution - *In Loco* Report	Start: 11/15/2010 Start: 11/22/2010	End: 11/20/2010 End: 12/03/2010
Claimant: Ministry of Health/ SCTIE		
Shape: Direct		
Object: Pharmaceutical Assistance [Popular Pharmacy [Brazilian Popular Pharmacy Program]]		

Source: Own preparation (2015).

Table 2 - Identification and basic data from audit No. 11357 of the Farmácia Popular do Brasil Program in the city of Fortaleza-CE.

AUDIT NO.: 11357		
Identification data		
Unit: Antonio Pereira de Barros	Municipality: Fortaleza	State: Ceará
Basic data		
Purpose: Audit of the Brazilian Popular Pharmacy Program		
Phase: Execution - *05* Loco Start: 02/09/2011 End: 05/13/2011 Report Start: 05/23/2011 End: 06/06/2011		
Claimant: Ministry of Health/SCTIE		
Shape: Direct		
Object: Popular Pharmacy		

Source: Own preparation (2015).

Table 3 - Identification and basic data from audit No. 11358 of the Farmácia Popular do Brasil Program in the municipality of Fortaleza-CE.

AUDIT NO.: 11358		
Identification data		
Unit: Maria Vieira Lira Barros	Municipality: Fortaleza	State: Ceará
Basic data		
Purpose: Audit of the Brazilian Popular Pharmacy Program		
Phase: Execution - *2nd loci* Start: 05/16/2011 End: 05/20/2011 Start: 05/23/2011 End: 06/03/2011		
Claimant: Ministry of Health/ SCTIE		
Shape: Direct		
Object: Popular Pharmacy		

Source: Own preparation (2015).

Table 4 - Identification and basic data from audit No. 11527 of the Farmácia Popular do Brasil Program in the municipality of Fortaleza-CE.

AUDIT NO.: 11527		
Identification data		
Unit: Santafarma San Antonio Farmacêutica LTDA	Municipality: Fortaleza	State: Ceará
Basic data		
Purpose: Audit of the Brazilian Popular Pharmacy Program		
Phase: Analytical Start: 07/04/2011 End: 07/08/2011 Execution -/w/oco Start: 07/11/2011 End: 07/15/2011 Report Start: 07/18/2011End: 07/22/2011		
Plaintiff: Mistério da Saúde/ SCTIE		
Shape: Direct		
Object: Popular Pharmacy		

Source: Own preparation (2015).

Table 5 - Identification and basic data from audit No. 12401 of the Farmácia Popular do Brasil Program in the city of Fortaleza-CE.

AUDIT NO.: 12401		
Identification data		
Unit: Enterprise Pay Less S/A	Municipality: Fortaleza	State: Ceará
Basic data		
Purpose: Audit of the Program here you have Farmácia Popular		
Phase: Analytical Start: 06/04/2012 End: 06/08/2012 Execution -/w/oco Start: 06/11/2012 End: 06/15/2012 Report Start: 06/18/2012 End: 06/29/2012		
Claimant: Federal Component of the National Audit System		
Shape: Direct		
Object: Pharmaceutical Assistance		

Source: Own preparation (2015).

Table 6 - Identification and basic data from audit No. 12406 of the Farmácia Popular do Brasil Program in the city of Fortaleza-CE.

AUDIT NO.: 12406		
Identification data		
Unit: Enterprise Pay less	Municipality: Fortaleza	State: Ceará
Basic data		
Purpose: Carry out an audit of the Aqui tem Farmácia Popular program		
Phase: Analytical Start: 05/30/2012End: 06/08/2012 Execution - *It Tco* Start: 06/11/2012End: 06/15/2012 Report Start: 06/18/2012 End: 06/22/2012		
Claimant: Federal Component of the National Audit System		
Shape: Direct		
Object: Pharmaceutical Assistance [Popular Pharmacy [Brazilian Popular Pharmacy Program]]		

Source: Own preparation (2015).

Table 7 - Identification and basic data from audit No. 12912 of the Farmácia Popular do Brasil Program in the city of Fortaleza-CE.

AUDIT NO.: 12912		
Identification data		
Unit: K. Martins Gonçalves - ME - Drug Pharmacy	Municipality: Fortaleza	State: Ceará
Basic data		
Purpose: Evaluate here is a popular pharmacy		
Phase: Analytical	Start: 12/17/2011	End: 12/21/2011
Report	Start: 01/07/2013	End: 01/11/2013

Claimant: Federal Component of the National Audit System
Shape: Direct
Object: Pharmaceutical Assistance [Popular Pharmacy [Brazilian Popular Pharmacy Program]]

Source: Own preparation (2015).

5.2 FINDINGS FROM AUDIT REPORTS

Report No. 10727 found that the company Santa Branca Empreendimentos Farmacêuticos Ltda, carried out actions under the Brazilian Popular Pharmacy Program in disagreement with the standards established by the Ministry of Health, Ordinance No. 971, of 15/05/2012, with regard to the dispensing of medicines based on medical prescriptions with no date of issue, prescription signed by a nursing professional, dispensing to people other than those registered on the medical prescriptions and linked coupons and lack of user signature on the linked coupons, in addition to prescriptions being presented illegible medical documents and without the medical professional's stamp.

The methodology used for analysis in report No. 10727 was to consult the National Health Fund website to verify the transfer of resources to the drugstore, analysis of transactions carried out, such as: medicines dispensed, amounts paid, medical professionals responsible for prescriptions, analysis of tax and linked coupons issued in the months of July 2007, June 2008 and March and September 2010 and carrying out home visits in order to interview users with records of purchasing medicines from the program at the aforementioned drugstore.

Table 8 - Summary of the Audit Findings of report No. 10727 of the Farmácia Popular do Brasil Program in the municipality of Fortaleza-CE.

Identification	Finding/Evidence	Conformity	Accepted
No. 124580	Registration of the Santa Branca Empreendimentos	According to	

	Farmacêutico Ltda pharmacy, updated with the Ministry of Health.		
No. 124585	Presentation by the pharmacy Santa Branca Empreendimentos Farmacêutico Ltda, of the mandatory documentation accredited by the Farmácia Popular do Brasil Program.	According to	
No. 124588	The establishment is identified in accordance with the Mystery of Health standards.	According to	
No. 124591	Lack of presentation of all	Non-conforming	Provided justification -
	tax and linked coupons for the month of June 2008.		Final opinion (No)
No. 124595	Lack of user signature on the linked coupon, in violation of the standards established by the Ministry of Health.	Non-conforming	Provided justification - Final opinion (No)
No. 124596	Coupons linked to subscriptions not belonging to medication users.	Non-conforming	Provided justification - Final opinion (Yes)
No. 124597	Dispensing of medicines based on medical prescriptions with no date of issue, in violation of Ordinance/Public Prosecutor's Office No.	Non-conforming	Provided justification - Final opinion (No)

	3,089/2009.		
No. 124598	Dispensing of medicines based on medical prescriptions without the medical professional's stamp, in violation of Ordinance/Public Prosecutor's Office No. 3,089/2009.	Non-conforming	Provided justification - Final opinion (Yes)
No. 124599	Prescription-based drug dispensing	Non-conforming	Presented justification - Final opinion
	signed by a nursing professional.		(No)
No. 124600	Presentation of copies of illegible medical prescriptions, in violation of the standards established by the Ministry of Health.	Non-conforming	Provided justification - Final opinion (Yes)
No. 124601	Record of medication dispensing from the program for the legal guardian and employee of Farmácia Santa Branca Empreendimentos Ltda, who declared that they did not use them.	Non-conforming	Provided justification - Final opinion (Yes)
No. 124655	Free dispensing of medicines from the program that does not comply with the standards established by the Ministry of Health.	Non-conforming	Provided justification - Final opinion (No)

No. 124656	Transporting users by Farmácia Santa Branca Empreendimentos Ltda.	Non-conforming	Provided justification - Final opinion (No)

Source: Own preparation (2015).

Report No. 11357 found that the company Antonio Pereira Barros carried out the actions of the Farmácia Popular do Brasil program in disagreement with the standards established by the Ministry of Health Ordinance No. 971 , of 15/05/2012, with regard to dispensing: with free purchase of medicines, based on an illegible medical prescription, and with coupons linked to signatures not belonging to the patients or without their signature.

The methodology used for analysis in report No. 11357 was to consult the National Health Fund website to verify the transfer of resources to the drugstore, analysis of transactions carried out, such as: medicines dispensed, amounts paid, medical professionals responsible for prescriptions, analysis of tax and linked coupons issued in October 2010 and carrying out home visits in order to interview users with records of purchasing medicines from PFPB. Having legal support, in law no. 8,080, of 09/19/1990; Decree No. 5,090, 05/20/2004; Ordinance No. 184, of 02/03/2011 and Ordinance No. 3,089, of 12/11/2013.

Table 9 - Summary of the Audit Findings of report No. 11357 of the Farmácia Popular do Brasil Program in the municipality of Fortaleza-CE.

Identification	Finding/Evidence	Conformity	Accepted
No. 153369	The Company's registration is updated with the Ministry of Finance	According to	-
No. 153255	The Company's registration is updated with the Ministry of Finance	Non-conforming	Provided justification - Final opinion (Yes)
No. 153478	Documentation of authorization to	Non-conforming	Provided justification -

	operation of Health Audit		Final opinion (Yes)
No. 153492	The company Antonio Pereira de Barros (Drogaria Progresso) presented a Certificate of Regularity from the Federal Pharmacy Council of the State of Ceará, CRF-CE for the year 2011.	According to	
No. 153808	Progresso drugstore did not present a Debt Clearance Certificate to the Ministry of Social Security, requested by the audit team through CA no. 01/2011.	Non-conforming	Provided justification - Final opinion (Yes)
No. 153512	Free dispensing of medicines	Non-conforming	Provided justification - Final opinion (No)
No. 153517	Presentation of an illegible copy of a medical prescription	Non-conforming	Provided justification - Final opinion (No)
No. 153371	Lack of user signature on the linked coupon	Non-conforming	Provided justification - Final opinion (No)
No. 153373	Coupons linked with subscriptions not belonging to medication users	Non-conforming	Presented justification - Final opinion (No)
No. 153264	The establishment is not displaying the identification of the Popular Pharmacy	According to	-

	Program in accordance with the standards established by the Ministry of Health		

Source: Own preparation (2015).

Report No. 11358 found that the company Maria Vieira Lira Barros carried out the actions of the Popular Pharmacy Program of Brazil in disagreement with the standards set by the Ministry of Health Ordinance No. 971 , of 02/15/2012, with regard to dispensing with based on medical prescriptions without the seal of the medical professional, with coupons linked to signatures not belonging to the users of the medicines or without their signature.

The methodology used for analysis in report No. 11358 was to consult the National Health Fund website to verify the transfer of resources to the Maria Vieira Lira Barro Company (Farmácia Popular do Povo) analysis of transactions carried out, such as: medicines dispensed, amounts paid, medical professionals responsible for prescriptions, analysis of tax and related coupons issued in October 2010 and carrying out home visits in order to interview users with records of purchasing medicines from the PFPB. Having legal support, in law no. 8,080, of 09/19/1990; By decree No. 5,090, 05/20/2004; Ordinance No. 184, of 02/03/2011 and Ordinance No. 3,089, of 12/11/2003.

Table 10 - Summary of the Audit Findings of report No. 11358 of the Farmácia Popular do Brasil Program in the municipality of Fortaleza-CE.

Identification	Finding/Evidence	Conformity	Accepted
No. 153076	Updated company registration	According to	
No. 154455	Certificate of Regularity presented to the Regional Pharmacy Council	According to	
No. 154459	The company's registration is not updated	Non-conforming	Provided justification - Final

	with the Ministry of Health		opinion (Yes)
No. 154463	Did not present Clearance Certificate of Debt from the Ministry of pension	Non-conforming	Provided justification - Final opinion (Yes)
No. 154466	No document was pre sented operation of Health authority not presented.	Non-conforming	Provided justification - Final opinion (Yes)
No. 153078	Lack of user signature on the linked coupon.	Non-conforming	Provided justification - Final opinion (No)
No. 153081	Coupons linked with subscription not	Non-conforming	Provided justification -
	belonging to the users of medicines		Final opinion (No)
No. 153107	The establishment is not exposing the identification of the Pharmacy Program Popular in accordance with standards established by Ministry of Health	According to	
No. 153238	Dispensing of medicines with based on medical prescriptions without a professional medical stamp	Non-conforming	Provided justification - Final opinion (No)

Source: Own preparation (2015).

Report No. 11527 found that the company SANTAFARMA, Santo Antonio Farmacêutica Ltda, carried out the actions of the Programa Farmácia Popular do Brasil in disagreement with the standards established by Ordinance No. 184, of 02/03/2011, with regard to lack of copies of medical prescriptions; sales of medicines carried out by branches that are not regularized, without an operating license, lack of linked coupon, sale of medicines to people whose names have not been confirmed, linked coupons with signatures not belonging to the users and lack of user signature on the coupon linked and part of the tax and linked coupons.

The methodology used for analysis in report no. 11527 was the analysis of linked coupons issued by the company in February 2011, and home visits, in order to verify the compliance of dispensations through interviews with people with records of purchasing medicines in the SANFARMA, Santo Antônio Farmacêutica Ltda and compatibility with that demonstrated by the Consolidated Transactions Report by CPF, issued by the department of Pharmaceutical Assistance and Strategic Inputs - DAF/MS.

Table 11 - Summary of the Audit Findings of report No. 11527 of the Brazilian Popular Pharmacy Program in the municipality of Fortaleza-CE.

Identification	Finding/Evidence	Conformity	Accepted
No. 158816	Lack of copies of medical prescriptions for the month of February 2011.	Non-conforming	Provided justification - Final opinion (No)
No. 159759	Branches without operating license. Private units - Here you have Popular Pharmacy.	Non-conforming	Provided justification - Final opinion (No)
No. 159051	Failure to present copies of health permits.	Non-conforming	Provided justification - Final opinion (No)

No. 160055	Copies of the linked tax coupons were not presented. Private Units - here is a Popular Pharmacy.	Non-conforming	Provided justification - Final opinion (No)
No. 159718	Medicines sold in the name of users not confirmed in interviews. Units	Non-conforming	Provided justification - Final opinion (No)
	Private - here is a Popular Pharmacy.		
No. 159739	Sell of no medications confirmed by users indicated on the tax coupons. Private Units - here is a Popular Pharmacy.	Non-conforming	Provided justification - Final opinion (No)
No. 159765	Sales of medicines through branches accreditation for the program. Private Units - here is a Popular Pharmacy.	Non-conforming	Provided justification - Final opinion (No)
No. 182863	Coupons linked with subscriptions do not belonging to the users of medicines. Private Units - here is a Popular Pharmacy.	Non-conforming	Provided justification - Final opinion (No)

Source: Own preparation (2015).

Report No. 12401 found that the organization Empreendimento Pague Menos SA, Farmácia Pague Menos, branch No. 31, carried out the actions of the Farmácia Popular do Brasil Program in disagreement with the standards established by the Ministry of Health, Ordinance No. 971, of 15 /05/2012, with regard to linked coupons without the beneficiary's signature, linked coupons signed by third parties without legal representation, linked coupons with the beneficiary's signature illegible, absence of medical prescriptions relating to the dispensation carried out in April/2012, registration coupon dispensing in the name of a person who declared that they had not received the medication.

The methodology used for analysis in report No. 12401 was to consult the National Health Fund website to verify the transfer of federal resources related to the program destined to the accredited pharmaceutical establishment, as well as the analysis of the Consolidated Transaction Reports and Data Reports. Individual, issued by the Department of Pharmaceutical Assistance and Strategic Inputs - DAF/MS and transactions carried out, such as medicines dispensed, amounts paid, medical professionals responsible for prescriptions and analysis of linked tax coupons for the month of April/2012, as well as the carrying out home visits in order to interview users who received medicines through the program.

Table 12 - Summary of the Audit Findings of report No. 12401 of the Farmácia Popular do Brasil Program in the municipality of Fortaleza-CE.

Identification	Finding/Evidence	Conformity	Accepted
No. 212905	Lack of presentation of tax/linked coupons	Non-conforming	The entity did not provide justification
No. 212907	Coupons linked without the beneficiary's signature	Non-conforming	The entity did not provide justification
No. 212915	Linked coupons signed by third parties without representation Cool	Non-conforming	The entity did not provide justification

No. 212921	Coupons linked without beneficiary address	Non-conforming	The entity did not provide justification
No. 212926	Coupons linked with incomplete payee address	Non-conforming	The entity did not provide justification
No. 211156	Absence of medical prescriptions related to the dispensation carried out in April/2012	Non-conforming	The entity did not provide justification
No. 212930	Coupons linked with illegible beneficiary signature	Non-conforming	The entity did not provide justification
No. 211468	Coupons linked without signature and address of beneficiaries	Non-conforming	The entity did not provide justification
No. 211470	Coupons linked without user address and signed by a third party without legal representation	Non-conforming	The entity did not provide justification
No. 211471	Linked coupons without beneficiary address and illegible signature	Non-conforming	The entity did not provide justification
No. 212984	Coupons linked without signature and incomplete user address	Non-conforming	The entity did not provide justification
No. 211473	Coupons linked to the beneficiary's incomplete address and signed by third parties without legal representation	Non-conforming	The entity did not provide justification
No. 211474	Coupons linked to the beneficiary's incomplete address and illegible	Non-conforming	The entity did not provide justification

	signature		
No. 211153	Inadequate provision of contraceptives to women under fifty	According to	-
No. 211155	Adequate dispensing of geriatric diapers for patients aged sixty years and over	According to	-
No. 213436	Beneficiaries interviewed satisfied with the way in which the Aqui tem Farmácia Popular Program is being carried out	According to	
No. 211127	Pharmacy registered with National Register of Legal person	According to	-
No. 213431	Employees who received medication use these products	According to	
No. 211136	The pharmacy has the advertising banner of the Programa Farmácia Popular do Brasil - PFPB	According to	
No. 211123	Presentation of Certificate of Regularity issued by the Federal Pharmacy Council	According to	-
No. 211137	Health record issued by the health surveillance of the City of Fortaleza in the process of renewal	According to	
No. 211130	Pharmaceutical establishment duly	According to	

	licensed by the Municipality of Fortaleza		
No. 211138	The establishment presented a Social Contract for the creation of the company Farmácia Pague Menos Ltda	According to	
No. 211132	There is no anti-counterfeiting sticker produced by the Ministry of Health in the pharmacy	Non-conforming	The entity did not provide justification
No. 213441	Registration of coupon dispensing in the name of people who declared that they had not received the medication	Non-conforming	The entity did not provide justification

Source: Own preparation (2015).

Report No. 12401 found that the organization Empreendimento Pague Menos SA, partially complied with the standards established by the Ministry of Health, Ordinance No. 971, of 15/05/2012, in the execution of the actions of the Farmácia Popular do Brasil Program, in the evaluation of its performance several improprieties were found regarding the dispensing of products, violating the rules of control and monitoring of the program.

The methodology used for analysis in report No. 12406 was the analysis of tax coupons and linked together with the respective medical prescriptions that demonstrate the sales and dispensations carried out by the establishment in April 2012, and their compatibility with the data from the authorization report consolidated from the Pharmaceutical Assistance department of the Ministry of Health/ DAF/ MS. The action was complemented with home visits, carried out to interview people who purchased items from the Program and signed the coupons linked to the company's sales records, as well as company employees who are also users.

Table 13 - Summary of Audit Findings from Program report No. 12406 Popular Pharmacy of Brazil in the city of Fortaleza-CE.

Identification	Finding/Evidence	Conformity	Accepted
No. 208166	Tax and linked coupons are filed in chronological order	According to	
No. 208329	The pharmacy is complying with the specifications and disclosures required to join the Program	According to	
No. 208530	Occurrence of dispensing of medication from the program for two employees	According to	-
No. 208172	Users served by the audited Popular Pharmacy Program of Brazil indicate satisfaction with the service	According to	-
No. 208312	Tax coupons signed by third parties without the authorizing document signed by users	Non-conforming	Provided justification - Final opinion (No)
No. 208524	The establishment has a responsible pharmaceutical technician	According to	-
No. 208316	Copies of archived recipes do not meet the conditions established by	Non-conforming	Presented justification - Final opinion (Partially)

	the Program rules		
No. 208352	Copies of medical prescriptions present several improprieties	Non-conforming	Provided justification - Final opinion (Yes)
No. 208104	The pharmacy registration with the Ministry of Health has been updated	According to	
No. 208546	The pharmacy has all the documents required for the operation of the company	According to	
No. 208181	Audited pharmacy employees consider that medical professionals do not comply with the standards of the Brazilian Popular Pharmacy Program when filling prescriptions	Non-conforming	Provided justification - Final opinion (Yes)
No. 208120	Linked tax coupons filed without the respective revenue	Non-conforming	Presented justification - Final opinion (Partially)
No. 208117	Linked coupons archived without user address record	Non-conforming	Provided justification - Final opinion (No)

Source: Own preparation (2015).

Report No. 12912 found that the company K. Martins Gonçalves, Farmácia Drogativa, carried out the actions of the Farmácia Popular do Brasil Program in disagreement with the standards established by the Ministry of Health, Ordinance No. 971, of 15/05/2012, in which refers to the dispensing of medicines in quantities greater than available stocks. In addition to crossing the information contained in the Consolidated Authorization reports issued by the Ministry of Health, and in the Death information system of the Ministry of Social Security.

The methodology used for analysis in report No. 12192 were the Manual Aqui tem Farmácia Popular; Ordinance No. 184 of 02/03/2011; Ordinance No. 971 of 05/15/2012; Audit Protocol of the Brazilian Popular Pharmacy Program No. 17 - Here you have a popular pharmacy - April 2012 version; Financial resources extracted from the National Health Fund (FNS); Activity itinerary (SISAUD/SUS System).

Table 14 - Summary of the Audit Findings of report No. 12912 of the Farmácia Popular do Brasil Program in the municipality of Fortaleza-CE.

Identification	Finding/Evidence	Conformity	Accepted
No. 242895	Lack of presentation of invoices containing the acquisition of medicines dispensed by the Brazilian Popular Pharmacy Program - PFPB in January 2012.	Non-conforming	Provided justification - Final opinion (Yes)
No. 242899	Presentation of invoices containing the acquisition of medicines dispensed by the Brazilian Popular Pharmacy Program - PFPB in February 2012.	According to	-
No. 242900	Lack of presentation of invoices containing the acquisition of medicines dispensed by the Brazilian Popular Pharmacy Program - PFPB in March 2012.	Non-conforming	Provided justification - Final opinion (No)
No. 242901	Lack of presentation of invoices containing the acquisition of medicines dispensed by the Brazilian Popular	Non-conforming	Presented justification - Final opinion (Partially)

	Pharmacy Program - PFPB in April 2012.		
No. 242902	Lack of presentation of invoices containing the purchase of medicines dispensed by the Brazilian Popular Pharmacy Program - PFPB in May 2012.	Non-conforming	Provided justification - Final opinion (Yes)
No. 242903	Lack of presentation of invoices containing the acquisition of medicines dispensed by the Brazilian Popular Pharmacy Program - PFPB in June 2012.	Non-conforming	Presented justification - Final opinion (Partially)
No. 242904	Lack of presentation of invoices containing the acquisition of medicines dispensed by the Brazilian Popular Pharmacy Program - PFPB in July 2012.	Non-conforming	Provided justification - Final opinion (No)
No. 242905	There is no record of medication dispensing from the Brazilian Popular Pharmacy Program for deceased people	According to	
No. 242893	Presentation of documents proving the regularity of operation of Pharmacy	According to	-

Source: Own preparation (2015).

Considering the irregularities presented in the audit reports analyzed, compensation was recommended to the Ministry of Health.

CHAPTER 6

CONCLUSIONS

In view of the facts presented, it can be concluded that many managers have little knowledge of the laws/decrees/ordinances in force. It is necessary to raise awareness, raise awareness, train managers and staff through higher health bodies and encourage the practice of continuing education so that they can carry out their activities, correctly complying with everything established by law .

It is concluded that managers do not have the knowledge of program standards to better execute them. The population must be the main agent monitoring the public management process through effective participation in decision-making management bodies, as they are the main consumers of the service, thus knowing their real needs. It is worth highlighting that health programs were created to serve the population.

The audit is an important management assistance tool, it identifies nonconformities and conformities in the management of services and educates the manager and the team involved to make decisions that strive for a quality public service. The audit is essential to detect problems presented in the services, through audit reports, which notify about inappropriate records of the actions of managers and staff, based on current laws, decrees and ordinances.

Continuing education activities represent a good strategy to be employed, especially if they lead the reports to reflect on practice and the possibilities present in daily work to improve the service offered based on quality and ethics.

In the field of assistance practice, a critical reflection on the auditor's role-function is necessary, regarding auditing not only as a tool aimed at financial and political interests, but also as a strategy in the search for quality of service and education of employees. managers.

Thus, for the health system to function in accordance with what is agreed and following all the principles and guidelines of the SUS, everyone must be involved in a committed and responsible way with public health and demand from professionals what they are responsible for so that the health system functions efficiently. Great challenges are posed for the consolidation of the SUS, many already overcome, others in the process of improvement, so the audit represents an instrument for achieving quality of care, guaranteeing a unique, universal, egalitarian, comprehensive and quality public health system.

CHAPTER 7

REFERENCES

BARBOSA, EC 25 years of the single health system: achievements and challenges. **Health Systems Management Magazine - RGSS** . São Paulo, v.2, n.2, p 85-102, Jul./Dec., 2013.Available at: < http://www.revistargss.org.br/ojs/index.php/rgss/article/view/51/102 >. Accessed on: April 10, 2015.

AYACH, C.; MOIMAZ, SAS; GARBIN, CAS Audit in the single health service: the role of the auditor in the dental service. **Health Soc** . São Paulo. v.22, n.1,p.237-248,2013. Available in: < http://www.scielo.br/scielo.php?sc ript=sci_arttext&pid=S0104-12902013000100021&lng=pt&nrm=iso&tlng=en >. Accessed on: May 10, 2015.

BRAZIL. National Health Council: Resolution No. 466, of December 12, 2012. **Official Gazette of the Union** , Brasília, DF, June 13. 2013. Section 1, p. 59, 2013.

______ . Ministry of Health: **History of health auditing.** Available at: < www.sna.saude.gov.br/historia.cfm >. Accessed on: April 17, 2015.

. Ministry of Health: **Decree No. 1,651, of September 28, 1995.** Regulates the National Audit System within the scope of the Unified Health System. Brasília: Ministry of Health, 1995. Available at: < http://www.planalto. gov.br/ccivil_03/decreto/1995/d1651.htm >. Accessed on: May 15, 2015.

. Ministry of Health: **Decree No. 5,090, of May 20, 2004.** Regulates Law No.

10,858 , of April 13, 2004, and establishes the "Farmácia Popular do Brasil" program, and provides other measures. Brasília: Ministry of Health. Available at: < http://www.planalto.gov.br/ccivil_03/_ato2004-2006/2004/decreto/d5090.htm >. Accessed on: May 15, 2015.

. Ministry of Health: **Decree No. 6,860, of May 27, 2009.** Approves the Regimental Structure and the Demonstrative Table of Commission Positions and Bonus Functions of the Ministry of Health, integrates the Professor Hélio Fraga Reference Center into the structure of the Oswaldo Foundation Cruz - FIOCRUZ, amends and adds an article to Annex I and amends Annex II to Decree no. 4,725 , of June 9, 2003, which approves the Statute and the Demonstrative Table of Commissioned Positions and Bonus Functions of FIOCRUZ, and gives other measures. Brasília: Mistério da Saúde, 2009. Available at:< http://www.planalto.gov.br/ccivil_03/_Ato2007-2010/2009/Decree/D6860.htm#art10>. Accessed on: May 20, 2015.

______ . Ministry of Health. National Audit Department of the SUS. **DENASUS - Federal Audit Management and the SNA** . Changes in the Federal Component, towards the Implementation of the National Audit System: problems, actions and results. Ministry of Health. Brasília: March, 2013. Available at: < http://sna.saude.gov.br/download/Relatorio%20de%20Gestao%20DENASUS%202002.pdf >. Accessed on: May 10, 2015.

. Ministry of Health: **Law No. 8,080, of September 19, 1990.** Provides for the conditions for the promotion, protection and recovery of health, the organization and operation of the corresponding services and provides other measures. Brasília: Ministry of Health, 1990. Available at:

< http://www.planalto.gov.br/ccivil_03/leis/l8080.htm >. Accessed on: May 10,

2015.

. Ministry of Health: **Law No. 8,869, of July 27, 1993.** Provides for the extinction of the National Institute of Medical Assistance for Social Security (Inamps) and other measures. Brasília: Ministry of Health, 1993. Available at: < http://www.planalto.gov.br/CCivil_03/leis/L8689.htm >. Accessed on: May 15, 2015.

. Ministry of Health: **Ordinance No. 184, of November 3, 2011.** Provides for the Brazilian Popular Pharmacy Program. Ministry of Health, 2011. Available at:< http://bvsms.saude.gov.br/bvs/saudelegis/gm/2011/prt0184_03_02_2011_comp.html >. Accessed on: May 20, 2015.

. Ministry of Health: **Ordinance No. 399, of February 22, 2006** . Announces the 2006 Health Pact - Consolidation of the SUS and approves the Operational Guidelines of the said Pact. Ministry of Health, 2006. Available at: < http://bvsms.saude.gov.br/bvs/saudelegis/gm/2006/prt0399_22_02_2006.html >. Accessed on: May 20, 2015.

. Ministry of Health: **Ordinance No. 971, of May 15, 2012** . Provides for the Popular Pharmacy Program of Brazil. Ministry of Health, 2012. Available at:< http://bvsms.saude.gov.br/bvs/saudelegis/gm/2012/prt0971_15_05_2012.html >. Accessed on: May 10, 2015.

. Ministry of Health: **Ordinance No. 3,089, of December 11, 2013.** Redefines the list of strategic products for the Unified Health System (SU S) and the respective rules and criteria for their definition. Ministry of Health, 2013.Available at: < http://bvsms.saude.gov.br/bvs/saudelegis/gm/2013/prt3089_11_12_2013.html >. Accessed on: May 20, 2015.

_____ . Ministry of Health. Secretariat of Science, Technology and Strategic Inputs. Department of Pharmaceutical Assistance and Strategic Inputs. **Pharmaceutical assistance in primary care: technical instructions for your organization** . 2nd ed. Brasília: Ministry of Health, 2006. Available at:< http://www.ensp.fiocruz.br/portal-ensp/judicializacao/pdfs/283.pdf>.Accessed on May 2, 2015.

_____ . Ministry of Health. Secretariat for Strategic and Participatory Management. **National Policy for Strategic and Participatory Management in the SUS - ParticipaSUS** . 2nd ed. Brasília: Ministry of Health, 2009. Available at: < http://bvsms.saude.gov.br/bvs/publicacoes/politica_estrategica_participasus_2ed.pdf > Accessed on: May 3, 2015.

_____ . Ministry of Health. Secretariat for Strategic and Participatory Management. National Audit System. SUS National Audit Department. **SUS audit: basic guidelines.** 1st ed. Series A. Standards and Technical Manuals. Brasília: Ministry of Health, 2011. Available at: _____ http://sna.saude.gov.br/download/LivroAuditoriaSUS_14x21cm.pdf > Accessed on: May 26, 2015.

_____ . Ministry of Health. Secretariat for Strategic and Participatory Management. National Audit System. National Department of

SUS audit. **Protocol 11. Intended for verifying compliance with the Health Adjustment Term.** Brasília: Ministry of Health, 2011. Available at: < http://sna.saude.gov.b r/download/PROTOCOLO-Termo_Ajuste_Sanitario-TAS-2011-09-22.pdf>. Accessed on: May 20, 2015.

_____ . Ministry of Health. Executive Secretariat. Undersecretariat for

Administrative Affairs. Department of Control, Evaluation and Auditing. **Auditing Standards Manual** . 2 ed. Brasília: Ministry of Health, 1996. Available at: < http://bvsms.saude.gov.br/bvs/publicacoes/manual_normas_auditoria.pdf > Accessed on: May 3, 2015.

CELLARD, A. **Document analysis.** In: POUPART, J. et al. Qualitative research: epistemological and methodological approaches. Petrópolis, Voices, 2008.

CLAUDINO, HG; GOUVEIALL, EML; SANTOS, SR; LOPES, MEL Audit of nursing records: integrative literature review. **Rev. infirm. UERJ** , Rio de Janeiro, v.21, n.3, p.397-402, jul./set., 2013. Available at: < http://www.facenf.uerj.br/v21n3/v21n3a20.pdf > . Accessed on: April 10, 2015.

DAYS, TCL; SANTOS, JLG; CORDENUZZI, OCP; PROCHNOW, AG Nursing audit: systematic literature review. **Rev. bras. sick.** Brasília, v.64, n.5, Sept./Oct., p. 931-937, 2011. Available at: < http://www.scielo.br/pdf/reben/v64n5/a20v64n5.pdf >. Accessed on: April 10, 2015.

FOPPA, AA; BEVILACQUA, G.; PINTO, LH ; BLATT, CR Pharmaceutical care in the context of the family health strategy. **Brazilian Journal of Pharmaceutical Sciences,** v.44, n.4, out./dez., 2008. Available at: < http://www.scielo.br/pdf/rbcf/v44n4/v44n4a20.pdf >. Accessed on: April 10, 2015.

GADELHA, CAG; MACHADO, CV; LIMA, LD; BAPTISTA, TWFHealth and territorialization from a development perspective. **Public health science** . Rio de Janeiro, v.16, n.6, p. 3003-3016, jun., 2011. Available at: < http://www.scielo.br/pdf/csc/v16n6/38.pdf >. Accessed on: April 10, 2015.

HELDER, RR **How to perform document analysis.** Porto, University of Algarve, 2006.

JESUS, WLA; ASSIS, MMA Systematic review on the concept of access to health services: planning contributions. **Collective health science.** Rio de Janeiro, v.15, n.1, pp. 161-170, Jan., 2010. Available at: < http://www.scielo.br/pdf/csc/v15n1/a22v15n1.pdf >. Accessed on: April 10, 2015.

Law no. 8,080, Organic Health Law of September 19, 1990. Provides for the conditions for the promotion, protection and recovery of health, the organization and operation of the corresponding services and provides other measures. **Official Gazette of the Union** 1990; 20 Sep.

LUDKE, M.; ANDRÉ, MEDA **Research in education:** qualitative approaches. São Paulo, EPU, 1986.

MACHADO, RR; COSTA, E.; ERDMANN, AL; ALBURQUERQUE, GL; ORTIGA, AMB Understanding the pact for health in the management of the SUS and reflecting its implementation. **Rev. Eletr. Nurse** 2009;v.11, n.1, p.181-187, 2009. Available at: < http://www.fen.ufg.br/revista/v11/n1/v11n1a23.htm >. Accessed on: April 1, 2015.

MENICUCCI, TMG History of Brazilian health reform and the Unified Health System: changes, continuities and the current agenda. **History Science. Health Manguinhos** . Rio de Janeiro , v.21, n.1, jan./mar., p.77-92, 2014. Available at: < http://www.scielo.br/pdf/hcsm/v21n1/0104-5970- hcsm-21-1- 00077.pdf >. Accessed on: April 10, 2015.

MINAYO, MCS **The challenge of knowledge:** qualitative research in health.

11th ed. São Paulo, HUCITEC, 2008.

O'DWYER, G.; REIS, DCS; SILVA, LLG Integrality, a SUS guideline for health surveillance. ***Public health science***. Rio de Janeiro, v.15, s.3, p.3351-3360, nov., 2010. Available at: < http://www.scielo.br/pdf/csc/v15s3/v15s3a10.pdf >. Accessed on: April 10, 2015.

OLIVEIRA, MM **How to do qualitative research.** Petrópolis, Voices, 2007.

PAIVA, CHA; TEIXEIRA, LA Health reform and the creation of the Unified Health System: notes on contexts and authors. **History science. health – Manguinhos** . Rio de Janeiro, v.21, n.1, p. 15-36, Jan./ Mar., 2014. Available at: < http://www.scielo.br/pdf/hcsm/v21n1/0104-5970-hcsm-21-1-00015.pdf >. Accessed on: April 10, 2015.

POLIT, DF; BECK, CT **Fundamentals of nursing research:** assessment of evidence for nursing practice. 7th Ed. Porto Alegre: Artmed, 2011.

PINTO, CBS; COSTA, NR; CASTRO, CGSO Who accesses the Brazilian Popular Pharmacy Program? Aspects of the public supply of medicines. **Science & Public Health.** Rio de Janeiro, v.16, n.6, p.2963- 2973, jun., 2011. Available at: < http://www.scielo.br/pdf/csc/v16n6/34.pdf >. Accessed on: April 10, 2015.

PINTO, CBS; MIRANDA, ES; EMMERICK, ICM; COSTA, NR; CASTRO, CGSO Prices and availability of medicines in the Brazilian Popular Pharmacy Program . **Rev. Public Health** . São Paulo, v.44, n.4, p. 611-619, Aug., 2010.Available at: < http://www.scielo.br/pdf/rsp/v44n4/1386.pdf >. Accessed on: April 10, 2015.

SÁ-SILVA, JR; ALMEIDA, CD; GUINDANI, JF Documentary research:

theoretical and methodological clues. **Brazilian Journal of History & Social Sciences** , n. 1, July, 2009. Available at: < http://rbhcs.com/index_arquivos/Artigo.Pesquisa%20documental.pdf >. Accessed on: May 1, 2015.

CHAPTER 8

APPENDIX

APPENDIX A - AUDIT REPORT ANALYSIS INSTRUMENT

Identification data

Audit No.: __________ Municipality:__________State:

Unit: ____

Basic data

Goal: ____

Phases

Operational - On-site ( ) Start:__/__/__ End:__/__/__

Analytics ( ) Start: __/__/__ End: __/__/__

Plaintiff: ____

Forms: ( ) Direct ( ) Integrated ( ) Shared

Object: ____

Findings

Finding number:______________________________

Item: ____

Finding: ____

Evidence: ____

Conformity: ____

Justification: ____

ATTACHMENTS

ANNEX A - RECOMMENDATION OF AUDIT REPORT No. 10727

VII - REGISTRO FINAL SOBRE A NOTIFICAÇÃO

As justificativas foram apresentadas por parte da empresa Santa Branca Empreendimentos Farmacêuticos Ltda. e devidamente analisadas pela equipe de auditoria, conforme registro no relatório final.

VIII - CONCLUSÃO

A empresa Santa Branca Empreendimentos Farmacêuticos Ltda. executou as ações do Programa Farmácia Popular do Brasil em desacordo com as normas estabelecidas pelo Ministério da Saúde, no que se refere à dispensação de medicamentos com base em receitas médicas sem data de emissão, receita assinada por profissional de enfermagem, dispensação para pessoas diferentes das registradas nas receitas médicas e nos cupons vinculados e falta de assinatura do usuário nos cupons vinculados, além de terem sido apresentadas receitas médicas ilegíveis e sem o carimbo do profissional médico.

A totalidade dos cupons fiscais e vinculados emitidos no mês de junho de 2008 não foi apresentada e, portanto, a regularidade das dispensações registradas nos referidos cupons não ficou comprovada.

Considerando as irregularidades constatadas, qual seja a falta de comprovação de regularidade das dispensações, o total de R$ 799,62 (setecentos e noventa e nove reais e sessenta e dois centavos) deverá ser restituído ao Fundo Nacional de Saúde, com os devidos acréscimos legais.

No que se refere à denúncia encaminhada ao Ministério Público Federal no Estado do Ceará relativa ao Procedimento Administrativo nº 1.15.000.001008/2009-51, que trata sobre a dispensação gratuita de medicamentos do programa e que instituições passaram a informar para seus associados que os mesmos receberiam gratuitamente os medicamentos da Rede de Farmácias Santa Branca, não necessitando se deslocar para os postos de saúde municipais, bastando para isso apresentar a carteira de associado, seu CPF e receita médica, a mesma é considerada procedente, haja vista que foi evidenciado em entrevistas com usuários com registros de aquisições de medicamentos do programa na Farmácia Santa Branca que a empresa realizava o transporte, ida e volta do Centro de Pesquisa em Diabetes e Doenças Endócrino-Metabólicas da Faculdade de Medicina da Universidade Federal do Estado do Ceará-UFC para a farmácia, a fim de que os pacientes recebessem os medicamentos e assinassem o cupom vinculado

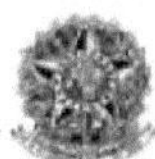

e, ainda, que o Centro de Pesquisas realizava a doação de valores que variavam entre R$ 0,25 (vinte e cinco centavos) a R$ 2,00 (dois reais) para que eles entregassem a farmácia no momento da dispensação, ou seja, o pagamento efetivamente não é realizado pelo usuário.

É o relatório.

VII - REGISTRO FINAL SOBRE A NOTIFICAÇÃO

Por meio do Ofício SEAUD/CE/MS nº 309, de 22/06/2011, recebido em 27/06/2011 (AR nº 945796028), o auditado foi notificado nos termos da Portaria DENASUS/MS nº 24, de 20/12/2004, conforme o direito do contraditório e da ampla defesa estabelecidos no inciso LV do artigo 5º da Constituição Federal de 1988. O auditado apresentou esclarecimentos/justificativas, através do Ofício nº 01/2011, contendo considerações quanto aos itens abordados nas constatações de não conformidades. A equipe analisou as justificativas e concluiu o relatório com as recomendações pertinentes para as justificativas não acatadas.

VIII - CONCLUSÃO

A empresa **ANTONIO PEREIRA BARROS** executou as ações do Programa Farmácia Popular do Brasil em desacordo com as normas estabelecidas pelo Ministério da Saúde, no que se refere à dispensação: com gratuidade na aquisição de medicamentos, com base em receita médica ilegível, e com cupons vinculados com assinaturas não pertencentes aos pacientes ou sem assinatura destes. Considerando as irregularidades constatadas, qual seja a falta de comprovação de regularidade das dispensações, o total de R$160,65 (cento e sessenta reais e sessenta e cinco centavos) deverá ser descontado do valor a ser pago pelo Ministério da Saúde referente ao mês outubro/2010.

É o relatório

ANNEX C - RECOMMENDATION OF AUDIT REPORT No. 11358

SNA - Sistema Nacional de Auditoria do SUS
MS/SGEP/Departamento Nacional de Auditoria do SUS
Relatório

Origem: SEAUD/CE **Data:** 22/06/2011 **Ofício Nº:** 318 **Data:** 22/06/2011 **AR Nº:** 945796155RL
Data de envio do AR: 22/06/2011 **Data de recebimento do AR:** 28/06/2011
Recebedor do AR: Gabriel Lira de Moura **Reitera Ofício Nº:** 318 **Data:** 22/06/2011

VII - REGISTRO FINAL SOBRE A NOTIFICAÇÃO

Por meio do Ofício SEAUD/CE/MS nº 318, de 22/06/2011, recebido em 28/06/2011 (AR nº 945796155RL), o auditado foi notificado nos termos da Portaria DENASUS/MS nº 24, de 20/12/2004, conforme o direito do contraditório e da ampla defesa estabelecidos no inciso LV do artigo 5º da Constituição Federal de 1988. O auditado apresentou esclarecimentos/justificativas, através do Ofício nº 01/2011, contendo considerações quanto aos itens abordados nas constatações de não conformidades. A equipe analisou as justificativas e concluiu o relatório com as recomendações pertinentes para as justificativas não acatadas.

VIII - CONCLUSÃO

A empresa **MARIA VIEIRA LIRA BARROS** (Farmácia Popular do Povo) executou as ações do Programa Farmácia Popular do Brasil em desacordo com as normas estabelecidas pelo Ministério da Saúde, no que se refere à dispensação: com base em receitas médicas sem carimbo do profissional médico, com cupons vinculados com assinaturas não pertencentes aos usuários dos medicamentos ou sem assinatura destes. Considerando as irregularidades constatadas, qual seja a falta de comprovação de regularidade das dispensações, o total de R$ 563,22 (quinhentos e sessenta e três reais e vinte e dois centavos) deverá ser descontado do valor a ser pago pelo Ministério da Saúde referente ao mês outubro de 2010.
É o relatório.

ANNEX D - RECOMMENDATION OF AUDIT REPORT No. 11527

VII - REGISTRO FINAL SOBRE A NOTIFICAÇÃO

O auditado foi notificado por meio do Ofício n° 355-SEAUD/CE, de 4/8/2011, nos termos da Portaria DENASUS/MS n° 24, de 20/12/2004, consoante o direito do contraditório e da ampla defesa, conforme o estabelecido no Inciso LV do Art. 5° da Constituição Federal de 1988, não tendo apresentado esclarecimentos/justificativas. Após análise, a equipe de auditoria teceu recomendações para as constatações de não conformidade.

VIII - CONCLUSÃO

A SANFARMA Santo Antonio Farmacêutica Ltda. executou as ações do Programa Farmácia Popular do Brasil em desacordo com as normas estabelecidas pela Portaria MS/GM n° 184, de 3/2/2011, no que se refere: falta das cópias das prescrições médicas; vendas de medicamentos realizadas pelas filiais que não se encontram regularizadas, sem alvará de funcionamento; falta de cupom vinculado; venda de medicamentos a pessoas cujos nomes não foram confirmados; cupons vinculados com assinaturas não pertencentes aos usuários e falta de assinatura do usuário no cupom vinculado; parte dos cupons fiscais e vinculados.

Considerando que o pagamento relativo à competência fevereiro de 2011 não foi efetuado pelo Ministério da Saúde, o Departamento de Assistência Farmacêutica e Insumos Estratégicos/DAF/SCTIE/MS não deverá efetuar o pagamento da quantia de R$24.689,27 (vinte e quatro mil, seiscentos e oitenta e nove reais, vinte e sete centavos), haja vista não ter sido comprovada a regularidade das dispensações.

Tendo em vista as irregularidades registradas, em especial o registro de dispensação de medicamentos vendidos em nome de usuário não confirmados nas entrevistas, faz-se necessário o encaminhamento do presente relatório ao Ministério Público Federal para as providências julgadas cabíveis por aquele órgão, nos termos do Artigo 3°, do Decreto n° 1.651/95, bem como ao Departamento de Assistência Farmacêutica e Insumos Estratégicos/DAF/MS para conhecimento e providencias que julgar necessárias quanto a Drogaria Sanfarma Santo Antônio Farmacêutica Ltda. junto ao Programa Farmácia Popular do Brasil.

É o Relatório.

VII - REGISTRO FINAL SOBRE A NOTIFICAÇÃO

Em consonância com a Portaria GM/MS nº 743, de 18/04/2012, foi notificada a responsável técnica, conforme apontamentos da presente auditoria, através do Ofício SEAUD/CE nº 507/2012, datado de 26/07/2012, encaminhado pelo Correio, mediante Aviso de Recebimento-AR, com data de 02 de agosto de 2012, para que a mesma manifestasse sua defesa, por escrito, em relação às não conformidades indicadas no Relatório de Auditoria. A farmácia auditada não apresentou justificativas.

VIII - CONCLUSÃO

A organização Empreendimentos Pague Menos S.A., Farmácia Pague Menos, filial nº 31, executou as ações do Programa Farmácia Popular do Brasil em desacordo com as normas estabelecidas pelo Ministério da Saúde, no tocante aos seguintes procedimentos: cupons vinculados sem assinatura do beneficiário, cupons vinculados assinados por terceiros sem representação legal, cupons vinculados sem endereço do beneficiário, cupons vinculados com endereço do beneficiário incompleto, cupons vinculados com assinatura do beneficiário ilegível, ausência de prescrições médicas relativas à dispensação efetuada no mês de abril/2012, registro de dispensação em cupom em nome de pessoa que declarou não ter recebido a medicação.

Outras incorreções foram identificadas, tais como: ausência de apresentação de cupons fiscais/vinculados, mudanças no quadro societário do contrato social da empresa sem a apresentação dos respectivos termos aditivos (211139), inexistência do adesivo anti-falsificação produzido pelo Ministério da Saúde (211132).

Os valores das impropriedades apontadas nas constatações: 212905, 212907, 212915, 212921, 212926, 212930, 211468, 211470, 211471, 212984, 211473, 211474, 213441, estão incluídos na proposição de ressarcimento atinente à constatação nº 211156 da não apresentação das prescrições médicas que soma R$39.126,15 (trinta e nove mil cento e vinte e seis reais e quinze centavos.

VII - REGISTRO FINAL SOBRE A NOTIFICAÇÃO

Notificado o gestor municipal da saúde por meio do Ofício/MS//SEAUD/CE nº 471/2012, de 3/7/2012, nos termos da PT/DENASUS nº 24/2004, atualizada pela PT/GM/MS nº 743, de 18/4/2012, consoante o direito do contraditório e da ampla defesa, conforme estabelece o inciso LV do artigo 5º. da Constituição Federal de 1988. O auditado encaminhou em tempo hábil suas justificativas para as impropriedades registradas, apresentando esclarecimentos e considerações sobre os fatos abordados. Após a análise, a equipe elaborou recomendações para as constatações cujas justificativas foram parcialmente ou não acatadas.

VIII - CONCLUSÃO

O estabelecimento Empreendimentos Pague Menos S.A. cumpriu **parcialmente** as normas estabelecidas pelo Ministério da Saúde na execução das ações do Programa Farmácia Popular do Brasil. Na avaliação do seu desempenho foram constatadas diversas impropriedades relativas à dispensação dos produtos, ferindo as regras de controle e monitoramento do Programa. Tais situações, descritas com a devida fundamentação

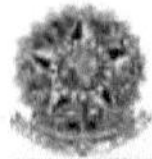

legal e encaminhadas ao gestor por meio do relatório preliminar, foram objeto de justificativas, apresentadas em tempo hábil, transcritas e analisadas. Os resultados da análise estão registrados nas constatações deste relatório final, com acatamento total ou parcial e alguns não aceitos, os quais geraram indicativo de restituição do valor de R$ 889,03 (oitocentos e oitenta e nove reais, três centavos), com os devidos acréscimos legais, ao Fundo Nacional de Saúde.

Em conformidade com a Portaria/GM/MS nº 971, de 15 de maio de 2012, este relatório deverá ser submetido à apreciação do Departamento de Assistência Farmacêutica e Insumos Estratégicos, para avaliação das impropriedades e aplicação das penalidades previstas.

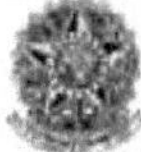

SNA - Sistema Nacional de Auditoria do SUS
MS/SGEP/Departamento Nacional de Auditoria do SUS
Relatório

Data de recebimento do AR: 28/01/2013 **Recebedor do AR:** Frtancisco Daniel Dias

VII - REGISTRO FINAL SOBRE A NOTIFICAÇÃO

Notificado a K.MARTINS GONÇALVES - ME FARMÁCIA DROGARIA, consoante o contraditório e da ampla defesa estabelecida no inciso LV, do artigo 5º da Constituição Federal de 1988, a responsável legal, a senhora Kleisa Martins Gonçalves, apresentou tempestivamente as justificativas das não conformidades elencadas neste relatório.

VIII - CONCLUSÃO

A empresa K. MARTINS GONÇALVES ME, FARMÁCIA DROGATIVA, dispensou medicamentos através do Programa Popular do Brasil em quantidades superiores aos estoques disponíveis (soma do estoque em 31/12/2011 e aquisições realizadas, entre 2 de janeiro a 31/07/2012) conforme detalhado nos Anexosj - I a VII - QUADRO DEMONSTRATIVO DOS MESES DE JANEIRO A JULHO/2012.

Além disso, no cruzamento das informações que constam nos Relatórios de Autorizações Consolidadas emitidas pelo Ministério da Saúde, e no Sistema de Informações sobre Óbitos do Ministério da Previdência Social, demontrados nos quadros dos meses acima.

Foram solicitados no Relatório Preliminar de Auditoria, justificativas sobre os fatos constatados, assim como, notas fiscais que comprovassem as aquisições do produtos ATENOLOL 25mg; CLORIDRATO DE METFORMINA 500mg e CAPTOPRIL 25mg, estes foram parcialmente apresentados, que reduziu o valor da Proposição de Ressarcimento inicialmente apurada.

Nesse sentido, considerando que as vendas de produtos sem estoque apuradas nos Anexosj - I a VII - QUADRO DEMONSTRATIVO DOS MESES DE JANEIRO A JULHO/2012, configuram-se como irregulares no âmbito do Programa, em desacordo com as normas previstas para o Programa na PT/MS Nº 184/2001, vigente até 15/05/2012, e a PT/MS Nº 971/2012, em vigência a partir desta data, a importância de R$4.669,20 (quatro mil, seiscentos e sessenta e nove reais e vinte centavos) deverá ser restituída ao Fundo Nacional de Saúde, com os devidos acréscimos legais.

Por fim, tendo em vista o teor do presente relatório, recomenda-se o encaminhamento ao Departamento de Assistência Farmacêutica-DAF para as providências cabíveis.

Printed by Books on Demand GmbH, Norderstedt / Germany